The Klutz Yo-Yo Book

The Klutz Yo-Yo Book

by John Cassidy

Klutz Press

Palo Alto, California

Grateful acknowledgments
are hereby made to:
Anne Johnson
Dennis McBride
Donald F. Duncan Jr.
Barney Akers
Tom Parks
Steve Gelb (for the nudge)
Wilf Schlee
Tom Kuhn
The Flambeau Plastics Company
Lindsay Kefauver
Rebecca Hirsch

Cover design: Vargas/Williams Design

Illustration: Sara Boore

Book layout and production:
MaryEllen Podgorski, Suzanne Gooding,
and Susan Robinson.

Yo-Yo manufactured by Hummingbird Toy Company,
Arcade, New York.

Klutz Press is an independent publisher located in Palo Alto,
California and staffed entirely by real humans. We would love
to hear your comments regarding this or any of our books.

Additional Copies

For the location of your nearest Klutz retailer, call
(415) 857-0888. If they should all be regrettably out of stock,
the entire library of Klutz books, as well as a variety of other
things we happen to like, are available in our mail order
catalogue. See back pages.

4 1 5

ISBN 0-932592-16-3

Contents

Yo-Yo Science 43

Yo-Yo History 57

et's say you took every yo-yo made and sold in the United States in the last 60 years and began piling them up, one on top of the other. At the bottom, you could start with the original Pedro Flores yo-yos that first appeared in Southern California in the early 1920's. On top of them, you could add the pre-war Duncans manufactured in Chicago, then would come a huge stack of Duncan 33's, 44's and 77's, carved in the Duncan factory at Luck, Wisconsin. Soon after that you'd have to add a pile of other brands —Goodies, Cheerios, and Royals at first, then the Festivals, followed by a huge mixed pile of premium yo-yos (a couple of million with the Coca-Cola logo alone). Add all the Duncan Imperials, Professionals, Butterflies etc. and then top it off with a thick layer of velvet, chrome, electric and miscellaneous models.

Now stand back.

Even if you left off a couple of million yo-yos— say all those that rolled down the sewer, or were eaten by the dog—you'd still have an impressive pile. Figure an average of one and a half inches each, you'd be looking at a yo-yo monument around 2,000 miles high, containing roughly half-a-billion "return top toys."

Afterwards, just for fun, you could take the strings off, tie them together, wrap them around the planet and take the loose end to the moon, where you could cut off the extra 40,000 miles or so and yo-yo-ize the earth.

1

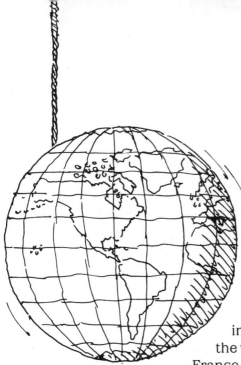

Actually, the earth was yo-yo-ized many years ago. The ancient Greeks started the process, but it received a couple of important boosts along the way. In pre-revolution France, for example, where the *emigrette* was a favorite pastime amongst the (soon to be un-landed) gentry. Across the channel, it was called the *quiz* and like many French imports, it was particularly well-received by those who took their cultural cues from the continent.

Elsewhere, in places as distant as Persia, Malaysia and the Philippines, yo-yos had long been a part of the popular street culture. Yo-yos, after all, are cousin to the spinning top, a nearly universal toy with ancient and hopelessly tangled roots.

It was left to Donald F. Duncan, though, an American entrepreneur with a P.T. Barnum flair for promotion, to firmly establish the yo-yo forever in the constellation of immortal toys. Looking at the aforementioned 2,000 mile high yo-yo monument, it would probably be safe to say that Mr. Duncan was directly or indirectly responsible for all but a mile or two of it.

How to Yo

"It's all very tricky."

In the world of yo-yo-ing, the tricks are everything. Just going up and down does not measure on the scale. Sorry. You can't even show your face really until you can throw a decent sleeper, one that lasts 4 to 5 seconds.

To get you started, cut the string to the right length. It should be about 3" above your waist when you let the yo-yo hang at the floor. Tie a slip knot and put it over your middle finger, just past the *first* knuckle (not the second, like rank amateurs). See the illustration.

After a while, the slip knot will tighten to the point that it feels as if it's cutting off your circulation. The end of your middle finger will look blue. This is normal. If you pursue the yo-yo trade long enough, with enough purity of purpose, you will one day develop a callous here. More than anything else, a true yo-yo callous is the mark of a Duncan pro.

3

Wind the yo-yo up and toss it down with a little bit of force. Use a back-hand throw per the illustration. The yo-yo will zip back up. Now try to soften the jolt that the yo-yo feels at the end of the string. If you can do this properly, the yo-yo will stick at the bottom, spinning. A little jerk, and it will come popping back up.

Throwing a sleeper like this is actually the first stage in achieving a condition which master yo-yo builder Tom Kuhn describes reverently as "The State of Yo." There's no defining it. You'll simply know when you get there.

Practice the sleeper toss until you can throw a hard spinner, with maximum rotation (it's all in the wrist) that sticks at the bottom for at least 4 to 5 seconds before it runs out of steam.

Adjusting the String for Sleeping

If the loop tightens up too much, the yo-yo will refuse to sleep. Look at your axle to see if the loop is twisted too tightly. If it is, let your yo-yo hang for a moment to unwind.

Tight. Won't sleep.   Just right.   Too loose.

Axle Knots: The Bane of Yo-Yo

When in the course of yo-yo gyrations the string gets tangled to the point that it knots around the axle, then it becomes necessary to loosen or cut the string inside the yo-yo, at the axle. *You have to be careful doing this*. If you scar the axle with a knife, your damaged axle will buzzsaw its way right through your string the next time you try a spinner.

Most experts agree that axle cuts have caused more yo-yo deaths than all other causes combined.

My recommendation is to use a ball-point pen, knitting needle or other suitably dull pointy instrument to work a loop loose inside the yo-yo. Then you can get a knife in there to very carefully cut the string.

The Basic Sleeper

1.

2.

This is where it all starts. The fundamental act of yo. Note that the toss is backhand, with your palm towards you. That way you can put some force into it. Nobody (but nobody) patty-cakes the yo-yo.

To get the yo-yo to sleep, make sure the loop is loose around the axle, then soften the jerk that the yo-yo feels when it hits bottom. (Practice). As you get better, you'll be able to really whip the yo-yo down, and still have it sleep at the bottom.

3.

Sleeping Beauty

3.

2.

This isn't actually a trick, so much as a labor-saving device. It's used to loosen or tighten the string around the axle. The idea is to throw a sleeper down at an angle across your body, then pull up on the yo-yo with your free hand so that it spins laying down flat like a lariat.

If the yo-yo is thrown to the right side of the body (as illustrated), the clockwise spin will tighten the string. If thrown to the left side of the body, the counter-clockwise spin will loosen the string.

4.

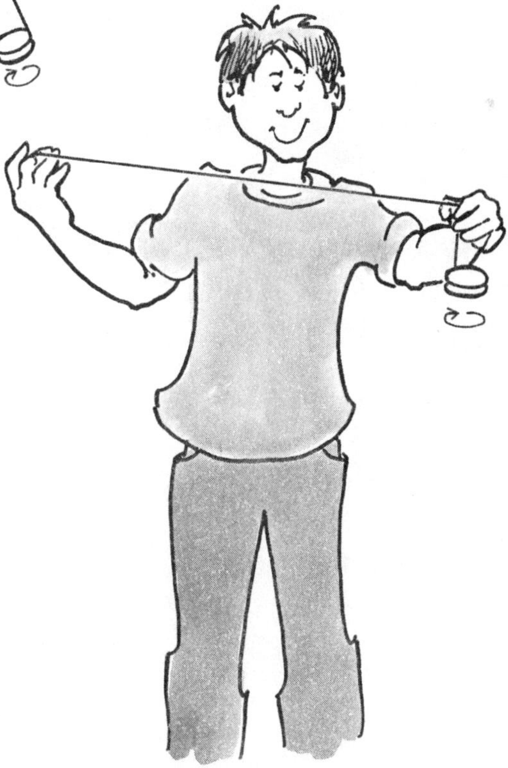

5.

Sidewinder

This is a variation of Sleeping Beauty. The only difference is that you do not pick up the string with your free hand.

1.

2.

Once you've learned these two "loop adjusting" tricks, you'll have to use them all the time. They're your tune-up tools. Use them any time your yo-yo won't behave properly—either because it sleeps too easily, or not easily enough.

3.

4.

5.

The Forward Pass

Another basic. Flip the yo-yo
out with a backhand throw
and when it comes back,
catch it palm up. A lot of
the tricks described further
on start with this move.

1.

2.

Walk the Dog

Abbie Hoffman once performed this trick in front of a House Sub-committee investigating some of his non-yo-yo hobbies and interests. According to the reports, Abbie walked his yo-yo the full length of the hearing room floor. Impressive.

1.

zzz

The trick is to throw a hard sleeper, and then gently set it down on a smooth floor. Then just trot along behind.

ZZZ

2.

Around the World

Throw a hard sleeper forward pass, then spin it around, sleeping all the way. Takes a loose wrist. At the completion of a full circle, a quick jerk should bring it back home. Make sure your string is loose enough around the axle. Not a good trick to do in a china shop.

zzz

Hop the Fence

Throw the yo-yo down (doesn't have to sleep), but instead of catching it on its way back up, let it flip over your wrist so it goes right back down. You can do this endlessly if you have a quick and flexible wrist.

If you're right-handed, this will gradually tighten the string. Lefties, just the opposite.

1.

2.

Loop the Loop

Yo-yo contests that ended in a tie were often settled with a loop-the-loop sudden death overtime. The contestants would each begin a series of loop-the-loops. The winner was the one who could stay with it the longest.

1.

It starts with a forward pass (no sleep). When it comes back, direct it over your wrist and then back out. Keep it to the inside of your arm, and like most yo-yo tricks—it's all in the wrist.

If you're right-handed, a lot of loop-the-loops will loosen the string.

2.

Reverse
Loop the Loop

Like the name says, the other direction on a loop-the-loop. One of the advanced stages in the state of yo occurs when you can do regular loop-the-loops in one hand, while simultaneously doing opposites in the other. This is a trick illustrated a little later on. Awesome.

Breakaway

Another fundament. Start as if you were flexing your muscle and throw the yo-yo out to your side. Swing it down in front of you (sleeping all the while) and when it comes up even with your chest, pop it back in.

The Breakaway is the starting move to a lot of advanced tricks. Don't forget to check the loop tightness if you can't get it to sleep.

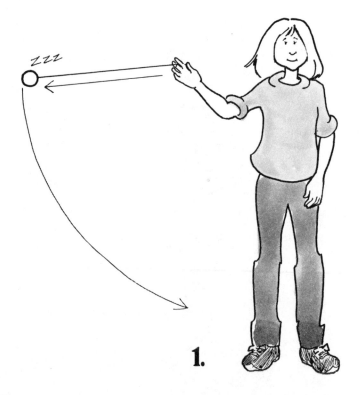

1.

zzz

2.

3.

Over the Shoulder

Throw a hard sleeper, then raise your hand to about your ear and put your elbow in front of the string. Then drop your hand down and tweak the string so that the yo-yo "wakes up" and flings itself over your shoulder.

Incidentally, the illustrations are about a thousand times clearer than these instructions.

1.

TWEAK THE
STRING

2.

3.

Pinwheel

Start with a Breakaway. In other words, begin by flexing your muscle and then throw a good sleeper off to your side. Check your loop tightness if you're having a hard time making your yo-yo sleep. Swing it by in front of you and then as it comes up on your other side, grab the string somewhere near the middle and execute some mini-round-the-worlds. The trick is to do it gently enough so that the yo-yo doesn't wake up. And when you grab the string, do it in such a way that your fingers don't get wrapped up in string as the yo-yo spins around and around.

1.

To finish up, let go of the string
and the resultant pop should
send the yo-yo back home.

2.

3.

29

Three Leaf Clover

This is a multiple loop-the-loop maneuver. Start with a skyward loop-the-loop, then use your wrist to re-direct the yo-yo back out in a regular straight-ahead loop-the-loop, then turn the next loop-the-loop down toward the ground. Finish up by directing the yo-yo out and then down.

1.

2.

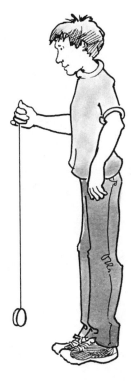

You never catch the yo-yo until the whole trick is over (it's all in the wrist).

Incidentally, if your yo-yo wants to sleep every time you throw it out, it just means your loop is too loose around the axle.

3.

Rock the Cradle

This is the basic among the "string" tricks. String tricks are "cat's cradle" kind of maneuverings, but done under the time constraints of a sleeping yo-yo.

1.

2.

Throw a hard sleeper and then look at the illustrations. Anything I could say here would only confuse you. You may want to practice this a few times with a "dead" non-spinning yo-yo, so as to get a feel for the hand placement. It'll take about 4–5 seconds to do this, so your yo-yo will have to be pretty well asleep.

3.

4.

Skin the Cat

This is another starting move kind of trick, used at the beginning of some more advanced things.

1.

zzz

2.

FLIP

Throw a hard sleeper and then, without waking the thing up, slide your free hand forefinger up the string to a midway point, so the yo-yo has to pivot around it. Then drop your hand and the yo-yo will finish in a forward pass, hit the end, and pop back. Supposedly.

3.

Trapeze

You cannot be taken seriously amongst dedicated yo-yo-ers until you can execute the Trapeze effortlessly. This trick is the threshold to the state of yo. It demands a high level of dedication and a loose loop around the axle.

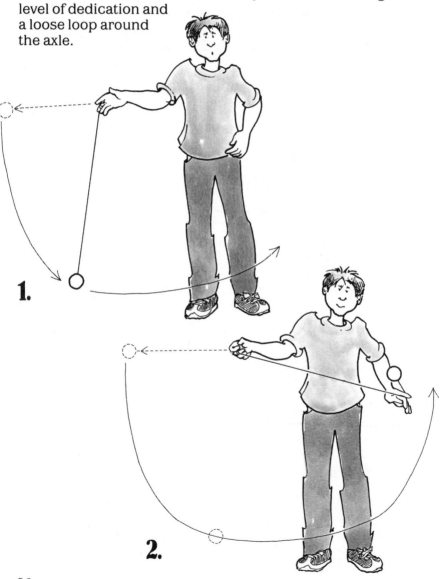

1.

2.

Start with a Breakaway. Flex your muscle, throw a hard sleeper out to your side and as it swings up on your other side, intercept the string with your finger about a foot or so from the yo-yo. As the yo-yo pivots around your finger, you have to catch it back on the string. This is hard. At first, it's impossible. But it can be done. Just takes a steady hand and dead aim.

Two weeks later.

Now that you've finally managed to catch the yo-yo on its string, bring your hands together as per the illustration and then spread them apart quickly, popping the yo-yo off and completing the trick.

Take a bow.

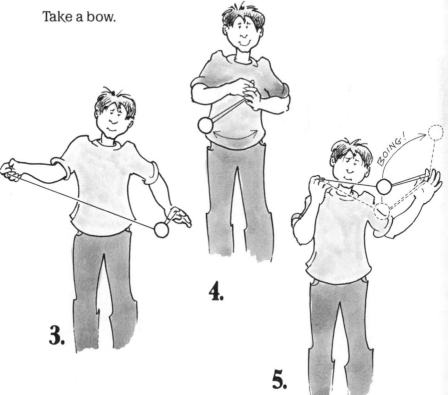

3.

4.

5.

Double or Nothing

This is a trick well into the land of serious yo. You'll have to be quite reliable on the Trapeze before you can plunge ahead with this one.

1.

2.

The idea is to throw a hard Breakaway sleeper, then intercept the string *three* times, catching the yo-yo back on its string as per the Trapeze. If you miss catching it (see last illustration) you've fulfilled the "Nothing" part of the title.

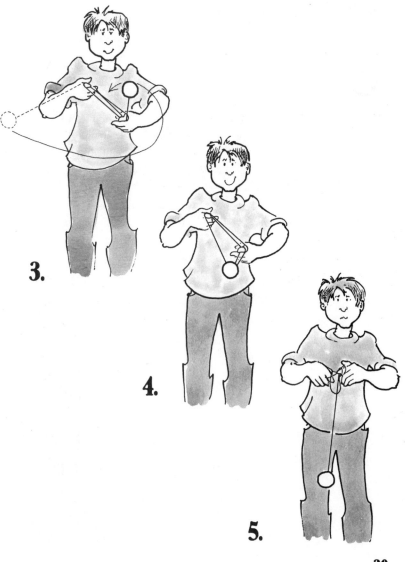

3.

4.

5.

Two Handed Loop the Loop

For all those who are ready to move beyond mere single yo-yo tricks, we include here a couple of tricks for the two-fisted yo-yo-er. You'll have to be an accomplished pat-the-head, rub-the-tummy sort of person before you can do either one of these.

& Milk the Cow

Note the Loop-the-Loop is done in opposite directions while the Milk the Cow is not. This is optional. It definitely looks more impressive to have the yo-yo's out of sync, plus it makes the motion easier. More like pedaling a bike.

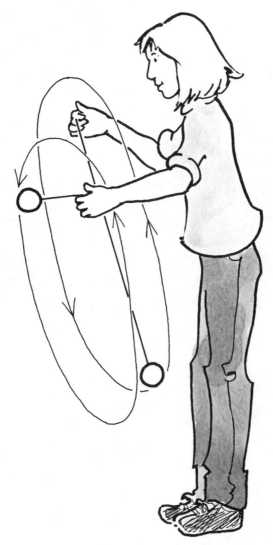

Yo-Yo Science

Although the motion and behavior of a yo-yo appears to be fairly simple—up, down, round and round—it is actually quite possible to turn it into a bewildering array of equations that derive from thermodynamics and Newton's second law. Those who choose to plow ahead with this section will never look at a yo-yo in quite the same way again.

But First, a Definition

Many of you, of course, have already been wondering: "Hey, what is a yo-yo, anyway?" Here then, is your answer: "A yo-yo is a body of rotational symmetry with a slender axle, which is allowed to roll on a flexible string."

Any other questions?

The second law of thermodynamics, to which we must now regrettably turn, concerns the conservation of energy. Neglecting the special case of atomic yo-yos, the energy given to a yo-yo when it leaves your hand *has* to go somewhere: either into the up and down motion (translational), round-and-round (rotational), or it is lost to friction against the air (not much) or the string (quite a bit).

In addition, as Isaac Newton so ably pointed out, any object in motion will neither slow down, speed up, nor vary from its way unless it is influenced by another force.

These are the constraints that a yo-yo is up against as it performs its various tricks, and these are the constraints that enabled Dr. Burger to analyze a yo-yo's motion. He discovered, for example, that a yo-yo is at maximum speed about halfway down its string. For the rest of its trip to the bottom, it is slowing down.

Wolfgang Burger is West Germany's "Dr. Wizard." A distinguished professor of theoretical mechanics at the University of Karlsruhe, West Germany, he has also been the host on a popular television science program for some years. Although Dr. Burger lists "nonlinear wave propagation" as his primary field of interest, he also confesses to a weakness for "physical toys." His analysis of yo-yo behavior has been published in both German and American scientific journals and represents the most in-depth treatment of the subject in print.

This last observation enabled Dr. Burger to pass judgement on a story which has been repeated in countless newspaper articles, magazine features, and nearly every yo-yo book ever written, i.e. the myth of the deadly Filipino hunting yo-yo.

Thinking About Going Hunting with a Yo-Yo?
Some things to keep in mind before you head out.

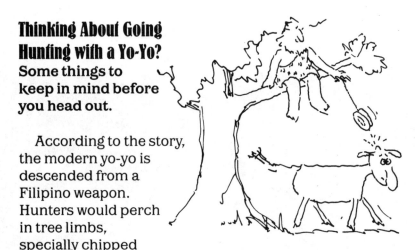

According to the story, the modern yo-yo is descended from a Filipino weapon. Hunters would perch in tree limbs, specially chipped flint yo-yos in hand, and wait for unsuspecting animals to pass below. If the first throw didn't work— no problem—it's a yo-yo! Just try again.

Unfortunately, as Dr. Burger's numbers point out, the unwinding string is actually a rather significant brake, acting to slow the yo-yo down and soften its impact at the bottom. From the prospective yo-yo hunter's point of view, this represents a serious shortcoming. (A second objection occurs to me. What if you miss? Then do you have a heavy, sharpened rock yo-yo hurtling up a string tied to your hand?)

Donald Duncan Jr. offers a plausible explanation for the source of the dubious "deadly hunting yo-yo"—mention of which appears in nearly every book on the subject.

"Tom Ives, my uncle, was with my father in the early days marketing yo-yos, and it could be that he started that idea. Probably embellished a rumor he'd heard."

"After all," Mr. Duncan explained, "he was a journalist."

Why Does a Yo-Yo Sleep?

A good question, since the answer gets to the heart of the modern yo-yo and makes possible the elevated "State of Yo" discussed elsewhere.

A yo-yo doesn't really roll up and down a string, it actually rolls up and down the inside of a loop of string. Unless the loop is twisted very tightly, when the yo-yo reaches the bottom of a properly executed toss, it will simply spin inside the loop. A little jerk, and the axle will catch on the string, and begin winding it up.

Pedro Flores introduced this loop innovation in his yo-yos in the early 1920's. Previous to that, yo-yos (i.e. quizzes, bandalores, discs and emigrettes) were primitive up-and-down only machines.

Can Modern Science Build a Better Yo-Yo?

This is the last question that Dr. Burger turned to, and armed with his calculations, he was able to isolate those factors that make the biggest performance difference.

Number one was weight distribution. A huge yo-yo with all its weight on the outside rim would spin for a much longer period. A couple of bicycle wheels for example makes a fabulous yo-yo (as was demonstrated once at MIT).

Number two was axle diameter. The skinnier the axle, the less friction it generates against the string (and, unfortunately, the quicker it breaks). A fat axle stores little of its energy in spin, falls very quickly, and hits with a great shock.

Number three was symmetry. When the yo-yo twists or wobbles it means that the weight is unevenly distributed, or that some twisting force (torque) is acting on it. Oftentimes this is the result of the string itself becoming too wound up.

Kinesthiology and Rotational Flymass Behavior in BIG Yo-Yos

As most students of yo-yo kinematics are aware, historical field work in the area has been exclusively conducted either on the surface of the earth, or within 2 or 3 feet of it. In addition to which, experimenters have invariably utilized the so-called "classical" yo-yo size and shape, i.e. smallish and incorporating no bicycle parts.

$$t = \int_0^t dt = \int_0^l dx/v(x)$$

In an effort to break with these conventions, while at the same time advancing our understanding of some of the more extreme forms of yo-yo behavior, my colleagues and I have recently concluded a number of kinematic experiments outside the 11th story window of our research facility. Inevitably, during the course of the experiments our apparatus traveled down to the 4th floor, back to the 11th, down to the 4th, up to the 11th, down to the 4th, up to the 11th, down to the 4th, up to the 11th... and so forth. Nevertheless, we were able to record changes in yo-yo behavior at these higher elevations, freed from the distorting effects of ground level gravity.

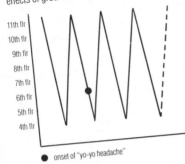

● onset of "yo-yo headache"

In addition, and for the first time, we incorporated a number of bicycle parts into our yo-yo apparatus. The photograph should be illustrative of both the apparatus and the experimental environment.

The results of the experiment confirmed an hypothesis first proposed nearly 2 weeks ago by ourselves as well as Frederick, Plotnick et al in Geneva: Firstly, bicycle wheel yo-yos are possible, but awkward. They are difficult to handle, troublesome to wind up, and nearly impossible to use for certain tricks, notably Rock the Cradle. We were forced to conclude that their commercial possibilities are limited.

Secondly, and perhaps more surprisingly, we discovered a new phenomenon directly connected with our decision to utilize a 16 lb. 3 foot diameter yo-yo. We have dubbed this phenomenon "yo-yo headache" and Drs. Shelton and Wiener stumbled upon it while leaning out the 6th floor window to record the yo-yo's behavior in its "going down" mode, as we called it.

The balance of our conclusions are best described in the language of analytical calculus and we turn with relish to that section now...

In the last 60 years more than 60 patents have been filed on "better yo-yos." Yo-yos have been designed that whistle, play tunes, automatically come back, glow in the dark, refuse to twist … etc. etc. So far though, the world has refused to beat a path to their doors, although Donald Duncan Jr. successfully markets a yo-yo (trademarked Pro-yo) that sleeps "50% longer" owing to better weight distribution.

Over the centuries, nearly every conceivable material has been employed in the making of yo-yos. Grecian "discs" were ceramic, Napoleonic "emigrettes" were ivory and brass, the classic Duncan "33" (possibly the most popular yo-yo in history) was maple, and of course, in recent years, we have seen the final degradation— plastic.

Harvey Matusow's Mysterious Stringless Yo-Yo: A National Security Threat or Not?

Harvey M. Matusow, a witness before the Senate Internal Security Subcommittee during the "McCarthy trials" of 1953, demonstrates the operation of his notorious "stringless yo-yo." Mr. Matusow, who at one point was being asked to describe the source of some of his money, pulled out his invention. When pressed about the details of his device, and the purposes to which the money from it were being put, Mr. Matusow abruptly took the 5th amendment. The entire episode made headlines the next day, but Matusow was unavailable to reporters. Questions about the stringless yo-yo persist to this day.

Although plastic is the
toughest substance, it really
doesn't have any "aerodynamic" edge over the earlier
materials. When Tom Kuhn began his search for the ultimate yo-yo axle material, NASA and various high-tech
chemical companies showered him with samples of
esoteric composite materials. After building nearly 100
different prototypes, Kuhn ended up right where he'd
started: wood.

"It just seems to work better,"
he says, "if you find the
answer why, let me know."

Yo-Yos in Outer Space

Sooner or later, everyone comes around to the same question: "Sure they're fun here, but what could I do with a yo-yo if I lived in outer space?"

Fortunately, modern science has the answer to that one in the person of David Griggs, an astronaut who took a specially fire-proofed yo-yo with him on the shuttle in July of 1984. Mr. Griggs was participating in NASA's "Toys in Space" program.

Discouragingly enough, Mr. Griggs discovered that yo-yos don't sleep in outer space. Astronaut Griggs (who got his yo-yo training from Tom Kuhn a few months before lift-off) found that his yo-yo, when it came to the end of its string, would never stick. The reason has to do with outer space's weightless conditions. In the absence of any gravity, the jolt given to the yo-yo at the end of a throw was plenty to send it right back up the string.

On the plus side, Lunar Loops and Round the World turned out to be much simpler.

Why Gyroscopic Stability Means So Much to Your Yo-Yo

(An Experiment *You* Can Do at Home)

1. Let your yo-yo simply hang on the end of its string.

2. Observe it begin to twist, or unwind. Make a note.

3. Now, with the same yo-yo, wind it back up and throw a sleeper. Why doesn't it continue to unwind, like it did before?

The answer, of course, is gyroscopic stability. A disc that is spinning (a yo-yo, a bicycle wheel... etc.) resists turning on any other axis but the one it's spinning on. The faster it spins, the more it resists. If you could mount a bicycle up in the air, spin the front wheel very fast, and then try the handlebars, you'd see what I'm talking about. Turning them would feel stiff. At some speed, they would nearly lock.

The scientific reasons are not very pretty, and I will leave them as an exercise. If it helps, nuclear submarines utilize the same principle (different equipment) as they navigate underwater.

Of course yo-yos generally don't spin fast enough to resist a serious degree of torque and many is the trick that has been foiled by a wobbling, tilted, or otherwise off-kilter yo-yo. Preventing this kind of wring axis behavior is a large part of the yo-yo-ers' trade.

Dr. Tom Kuhn dates it all from 1957, when he took a Detroit neighborhood yo-yo title in a Duncan sponsored contest. Weeks of diligent, finger-aching practice had finally paid off. First prize was a genuine rhinestone studded Duncan yo-yo, and Kuhn carefully stored it away.

In the years following, adult distractions intervened and stifled his career. College, dental school, a practice in San Francisco. It was a long diversion, but Kuhn finally got back on track in 1976 when a friend gave him a rosewood yo-yo.

"I hadn't seen a wooden yo-yo in years," he recalled, "and I was immediately taken with it."

Unfortunately, the axle on the rosewood yo-yo soon broke, and in the course of repairing it, Kuhn began to get immersed in the fine art of wooden yo-yo building. He began experimenting in his home shop with various woods and various shapes. It took years, but Tom Kuhn eventually became the nation's Stradivarius of yo-yo. His yo-yos, built in limited quantities, eventually gained a cult following. Each one is carefully machined, lacquered, hand-tested and branded. They are, by general consensus, the finest examples of the yo-yo builders art.

Although nearly all of Kuhn's yo-yos are a modest 3 or 4 inches in diameter, he was once stricken with the need to built a gargantuan model. The result is pictured here and was hoisted and successfully yo-ed from a crane in San Francisco. The Guinness people were duly notified and Tom Kuhn and his Big Yo can now be found under "Yo-Yo, World's Biggest."

Mirabeau Chef d'une Légion.
de l'Armée noire et jaune en grand uniforme.

Yo-Yo History

Trying to pin down the owner and location of history's first yo-yo is a foredoomed exercise. D.W.Gould, author of the definitive history of the spinning top, after attempting to verify a number of competing theories, concluded that the top (and its more refined cousin, the yo-yo) were independently invented by many people, in many places. My own theory is that the yo-yo was invented by the youngest kid of the guy that invented the wheel. I have evidence, too, although I am saving it for later publication.

History's first graphic evidence that the State of Yo existed in ancient times occurs on a Greek vase dating from 500 B.C. where a young Greek is depicted

in full yo-yo stride. Subsequent mention of the yo-yo is spotty until it reappears in full cry in 18th century France. Where and how it spent the intervening 2300 years seems to be an area ripe for speculation. The fabled Filipino hunting yo-yo may well offer a clue. Like most myths, it probably has a kernel of truth. Some writers have speculated that a retrievable (but non-yo-yo-ing) rock-on-a-string weapon may have existed in the Philippines—alongside the more benign toy—for millenia.

If such were the case, it would support the theory that the yo-yo, like the top, boomerang, footbag and other pre-historic toys, simply became embedded in the street life of dozens of cultures. Whether as in import, or an independently invented toy it hardly matters.

Its dramatic reappearance in 18th century France can be most directly traced to the Chinese version of the toy, probably imported, along with a number of other curiosities, by missionaries. A French minister of state at the time (Jean Baptiste-Berlin) was an amateur collector of things Chinese and his interest may well have given the new device an added boost.

The Paris Picayune

Sept. 14, 1789

Europe Goes Yo-Yo

Versailles. Spokesman from the Royal Court today confirmed the rumors that have been circulating around the palace for a number of days: the future King Louis XVII has finally been able to "Rock the Cradle" with his yo-yo. "Of course, we're relieved," said one source who chose to remain anonymous, "the littly tyrant was becoming even more irritating than usual. Maybe now that he's finally got the thing, he'll cut us a little slack."

In any event, the joujou or emigrette, as it was some-times called, soon needed no boost. It swept through French society with a Hula-Hoop's vengeance. The future King Louis XVII was painted (at the age of 4) in posses-sion of one in the year 1789. Clubs were formed, compe-titions held. It was a National State of Yo.

From France, it soon took over England and the rest of Europe. The Prince of Wales (the future George IV) was portrayed with his "quiz" in hand. As in France, it seems to have been a fashionable diversion, particularly popu-lar amongst the upper classes.

By 1824, however, it was a faded fad, described by one writer of the time as a "bygone toy."

But the little return top with the 2,000 year pedigree was not so easily dismissed. It may have dropped from fash-ion on the continent, but it was still destined for great things elsewhere.

In the U.S., inventors spent the rest of the century busily adapting and improving the device, hoping to re-kindle the same kind of fever last seen in France and England. The patent files are filled with their efforts, but none of them appear to have gotten much further than the drawing board. In the Philippines, meanwhile, the yo-yo continued to be a common toy familiar to everyone, including a youngster named Pedro Flores, who emigrated as a young man to the United States in 1920 where he took a job at a hotel in Southern California.

To his surprise, Mr. Flores soon discovered that no one in his new home had ever seen a yo-yo before. Perhaps even more surprisingly, he found that a few impromptu demonstrations with his little return top could draw a crowd. Mr. Flores, showing no lack of entrepreneurial spirit, soon began manufacturing the tops. Not long afterwards he applied for, and registered, the trademark—"Flores Yo-Yo." According to reports of the time, the Flores Yo-Yo Company was doing a small, but profitable little business in Los Angeles, when its product was spotted by a midwestern American businessman in 1927 by the name of Donald F. Duncan.

And things were never the same again.

Donald F. Duncan was an American classic. A born salesman with a sharp eye for product and a promotional genius. In Europe they'd call him nothing less than an American archetype and put his statue in a smaller wing of the same museum that held John Rockefeller, P.T. Barnum and Andrew Carnegie.

Born in West Virginia in 1892, Duncan had already amassed a small fortune by the time he was 30. He had been, by turns; a successful salesman for a candy company, co-holder of the patent on 4-wheel hydraulic automobile brakes, one of the first to develop "premium incentives" ("Kids! Just send in 2 boxtops and receive *free* one..."), the inventor of the Eskimo Pie, and the originator of the Good Humor ice cream truck. Later on, he would be one of the first to "popularize" parking meters. (At one time, the Duncan Parking Meter Company owned 80% of the U.S. market.)

But the product with which his name is irrevocably linked is, of course, the yo-yo.

In 1927 Donald Duncan was in California on business when his path crossed a yo-yo's for the first time. His initial impression, as he recollected later, was not overwhelming, but he did take one home with him.

The little top must have grown on him, because it wasn't too long before he was manufacturing his own in Chicago. A few years after that, he bought the Flores Yo-Yo Company, along with the "yo-yo" trademark, for a reported $25,000.

His initial efforts at selling his new acquisition met with little success. He tried advertising the toy, with discouraging results: "There wasn't enough volume." But Donald Duncan was not an easily discouraged sort. He had already experienced some earlier success selling chinaware via a "premium incentive" marketing scheme, and he soon dreamt up a way of doing the same thing with yo-yos. What he needed, he felt, was a lot of free advertising space in newspapers. What's more, he thought he knew where he could get it.

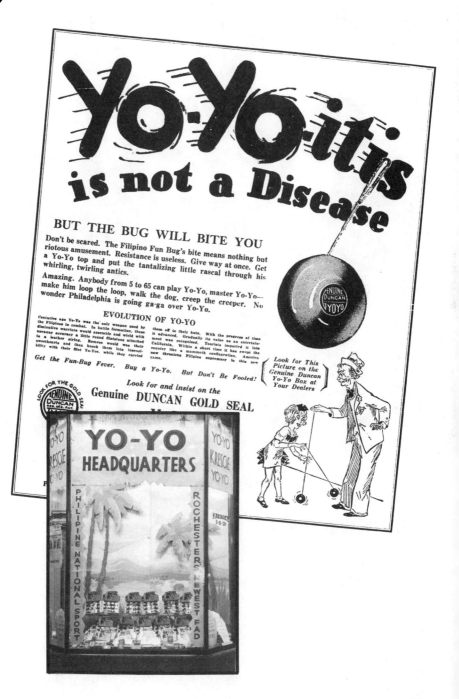

Yo-Yo-itis
is not a Disease

BUT THE BUG WILL BITE YOU

Don't be scared. The Filipino Fun Bug's bite means nothing but riotous amusement. Resistance is useless. Give way at once. Get a Yo-Yo top and put the tantalizing little rascal through his whirling, twirling antics.

Amazing. Anybody from 5 to 65 can play Yo-Yo, master Yo-Yo—make him loop the loop, walk the dog, creep the creeper. No wonder Philadelphia is going ga-ga over Yo-Yo.

EVOLUTION OF YO-YO

Centuries ago Yo-Yo was the only weapon used by the Filipino in combat. In battle formation, these diminutive warriors would assemble and wield with uncanny accuracy a little round flintstone attached to a leather string. Remorse would woo their sweethearts and then knock them into insensibility with their flint Yo-Yos, while they carried them off to their huts. With the progress of time it advanced. Gradually its value as an entertainment was recognized. Tourists imported it into California. Within a short time it has swept the country like a mammoth conflagration. America now threatens Filipino supremacy in this new game.

Get the Fun-Bug Fever. Buy a Yo-Yo. But Don't Be Fooled!

Look for and insist on the
Genuine DUNCAN GOLD SEAL

LOOK FOR THE GOLD SEAL
GENUINE DUNCAN REG. U.S. PAT.
YO-YO

Look for This Picture on the Genuine Duncan Yo-Yo Box at Your Dealers

YO-YO
HEADQUARTERS
YO-YO KRESGE YO-YO
PHILIPINE NATIONAL SPORT
ROCHESTER'S NEWEST FAD
KRESGE

GENUINE DUNCAN YOYO

Citizen Kane and the Yo-Yo

In 1930, William Randolph Hearst owned a chain of
papers scattered across the country. The newspaper
business was a cutthroat industry at the time, with nasty
circulation wars common amongst competing papers.
Hearst was already legendary for taking no survivors.

Duncan traveled to Hearst's palace in San Simeon
California where he talked his way past the servants and

got in to see the great man himself. His pitch was tailored and to the point: "I have a great plan to stimulate circulation," he said, "I can get new readers for your papers."

The idea was a piece of merchandising inspiration: Duncan would target a Hearst newspaper town and set up demonstrations and yo-yo contests. Prizes like bicycles, gloves, baseballs, etc. would be offered, but in order to be eligible to win them, the kids would have to bring in three 6-month newspaper subscriptions.

Hearst knew a good idea when he heard one. Duncan was given Chicago to try it out. All the papers at the time contained white space, unfilled columns that usually contained "fillers" of one sort or another. Now, in the Hearst Chicago paper, they'd contain "Duncan Yo-Yo Contest" announcements.

When Duncan went back to the managing editor with the idea he was told it would never work. Thirty years later he could still recall that prediction with satisfaction: "We brought in 50,000 new subscribers in that promotion."

Duncan soon moved on to more Hearst towns, supported by all that white space, the promotions caught on with flabbergasting success. One 30-day campaign in Philadelphia in 1931 resulted in the sale of *3 million* yo-yos. It was absolutely phenomenal.

In order to conduct the demonstrations and contests, Duncan hired Filipinos who developed a full repertoire of tricks with such names as "Walk the Dog," "Around the Moon," "Man on the Flying Trapeze"…etc. A small cadre of demonstrators was soon touring a country that was rapidly going yo-yo nuts.

A generation of kids,

those who grew up in the 30's era,
learned to anticipate the seasonal Duncan promotions,
with their touring yo-yo champions. According to Donald
Duncan's son, the demonstrators were paid $15 a week
and they made their schedules on the trolley. In their
own small way the itinerant Duncan yo-yo pro became a
small-town American icon, as familiar and reassuring as
the tent-shows and carnivals that followed the seasons in
Depression era U.S.A.

During the war years, yo-yos and yo-yoing
took an understandable hiatus, but no sooner
was it over than they came roaring back.
And this time,
Duncan had company.

A couple of former
Duncan demonstrators, having
split from Duncan for one reason or another, went into
business. Out of that came the Royal Top Company and
Cheerio, both of whom jumped on the yo-yo bandwagon
by 1946. They, together with a couple of smaller upstarts,
battled it out for America's yo-yo dollar during the rest
of the 40's and early 50's. Everybody used the same kind
of promotional contests and touring demonstrators that
had been so successful for Duncan before the war. It was
gloves-off market share competition, guaranteed to yield
casualties.

68

Cheerio was the first, they sold out to Duncan in 1954, and then another company, Hi-Ker went the same route a couple of years later.

Of course, one of Duncan's biggest edges during the "yo-yo wars" was the fact that they were the only ones legally able to even use the term. Everybody else had to get by on such vagaries as "come-backs," "return tops" etc. Duncan's lawyers were constantly in court beating back trademark infringers. It got so expensive at one point that they licensed the term to two other companies, rather than test it in court.

But, by 1962, when the yo-yo craze hit new heights, Duncan finally felt confident enough to force the issue. They sued their prime competitor, Royal Tops, for trademark infringement.

It turned out to be a grievous error.

The court ruled, after appeal, that "yo-yo" had been so commonly used to describe the toy in a generic sense, that the term had passed into the public domain. The court was also presented with evidence from linguists and anthropologists that "yo-yo" was not a Duncan coinage, but in fact the name of the toy in many languages— including Tagalog. It was a two-pronged attack with one bottom line: Anybody could use "yo-yo."

It was also the realization of a corporate nightmare. A trademark with wide recognition represents a piece of fabulously valuable property. The Coca-Cola Company, for example, maintains a small army of lawyers whose only task is to stamp out unauthorized use of the term "Coke." Even the hint of the loss of that trademark would be enough to send their executives to the window ledges.

"If it isn't a DUNCAN ...it isn't a YOoYO Top"

But the loss of their trademark turned out to be the lesser of the two problems that faced the Duncan Company in the early 60's. Far more serious was the condition of their balance sheet: they were foundering in phenomenal success.

The idea that a company could suffer a mortal blow by an unprecedented surge in the popularity of its major product strikes many as being a little paradoxical. But it's actually not at all unknown, particularly in the toy industry. When the Hula-Hoop craze hit the U.S. in 1958, their maker, Wham-O Corporation, sold a phenomenal 80 million of the things, and, in the words of their founder, "nearly went broke doing it."

Amongst veteran toy industry observers, the year 1962 means only one thing: yo-yos. The numbers were so big they didn't even make sense: Forty-five million units were sold in a country that had less than 40 million kids. Duncan's plant was running 3 shifts a day and still couldn't keep up.

The spark that ignited the fire was television. At a time when touring demonstrators was too expensive, the Duncan people turned to TV advertising. At first tentatively, and then with more and more confidence, they began running ads on children's programs. In startlingly short order, they were riding an out-of-control demand, paying air freight costs to get in more product, premiums to their wood suppliers for quicker service, overtime to their workers…and all the time throwing more money at their ad agency to keep the frenzy going.

Meanwhile, knowing they were running out of kids, Duncan spent a lot of capital adding different yo-yos to the line. Plus, they were investing in the expensive tooling in order to start the switch to plastic.

It was a wild ride with money flowing in and out at breakneck speed. Unfortunately, when the dust settled and demand tapered off, the outflow had outstripped the inflow. In 1965 the company listed assets of $650,000 and debts of $1,000,000. They filed for bankruptcy. In many ways, it was the end of an era.

The Up's and Down's of the Yo-Yo Over Fifty Years

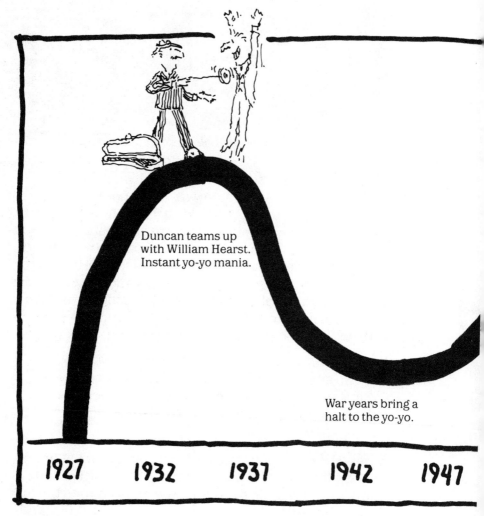

Duncan teams up with William Hearst. Instant yo-yo mania.

War years bring a halt to the yo-yo.

1927   1932   1937   1942   1947

Donald F. Duncan sees his first yo-yo.

The peak year—
1962. The Ultimate
State of Yo arrives
as 45 million yo-yos
sold in one frantic
season.

A mini-boom. Nash-
ville, Tennessee
(population:
320,000) reports
340,000 yo-yos sold
in one season.

Yo-yo comes roaring
back. Bigger pro-
motions, more
demonstrators,
more competition.
"Yo-yo wars" break
out.

Duncan loses
"yo-yo" trademark
and soon thereafter,
declares bank-
ruptcy. Flambeau
Plastics buys rights
to Duncan name.

1952   1957   1962   1967   1972

73

After Duncan

As the pieces of the Duncan pie were   auctioned off, probably the most valuable of them all—the Duncan name itself—didn't go until the end, when the Flambeau Plastics Company of Baraboo, Wisconsin bought it.

Bill Sauey, president of Flambeau, didn't share the general impression that yo-yos were dead and gone, a one-time fad that would rise no more. He saw a toy with long-term, steady potential. As a result, he plunged back into the business, putting out an array of plastic yo-yos under the Duncan name.

And history has borne him out. The basic year-in, year-out yo-yo sales have been more than enough to keep Flambeau in the business, and a mini-fad in the early 70's posted some impressive numbers. These days, the Flambeau Plastics Corporation is the major manufacturer of yo-yos, staging numerous tours and promotions. They market 4 different plastic models and sell enough of them to jealously guard their sales figures.

Whether or not yo-yos will ever rise to the heights they did in the 30's, 50's and 60's is hard to tell. Fads are the product of a tricky mix of mass craziness and fortuitous timing. It may be that the yo-yo has retired from the fad business and settled into the quiet respectability of a standard plaything. Or it may be that the next full-blown, nation-wide manic State of Yo is waiting just around the corner...

Abbie Hoffman, in 1968, during a break in his testimony before the House Subcommittee on Un-American Activities demonstrates "Walk the Dog," one of the tricks he used to win a Duncan yo-yo championship patch in 1958. Mr. Hoffman was before the committee in connection with some of his non-yo-yo interests and activities.

Bibliography

Books

Dickson, Paul. *The Mature Person's Guide to Kites, Yo-Yos, Frisbees, and other Childlike Diversions,* New American Library, 1977, New York. A compendium of facts and trivia about some of the toy immortals.

Flambeau Plastic Company. *The Original Duncan Yo-Yo & Spin Top Trick Book,* Flambeau Plastic Company, 1985, Baraboo, WI. This is the most recent edition of the little tricks booklet that Duncan has sold by the millions over the past 50 years.

Gould, D.W. *The Top: Universal Toy, Enduring Pastime.* Clarkson N. Potter, 1973, New York. Nothing more need ever be said about the top.

Malko, George. *The One and Only Yo-Yo Book.* Avon Books, 1978, New York. Easily the most complete treatment on the history of the yo-yo. Currently out of print, but check your library.

Olney, Russ. *The Amazing Yo-Yo.* Lothrop, Lee & Shepard Books, 1980, New York. Another in-depth volume of yo-yo tricks, basic to advanced.

Rule, Bob. *Yo-Yo Secrets.* Yo-Yo Promotions Inc, 1971, Atlanta, GA. Bob Rule is one of best known of the Duncan touring pros. This is his tricks booklet.

Zeiger, Helane. *World on a String: The How-To Yo-Yo Book.* Contemporary Books, 1979, Chicago. A complete treatment on all the yo-yo's trickery, by one of the few female Duncan champions.

Newsletters

Crump, Stuart Jr., editor. *Yo-Yo Times,* the first independent newsletter for yo-yo-lovers of all ages. $12/year. Send for sample copy. *Yo-Yo Times,* Creative Communications, Inc., P.O. Box 1519, Dept. KB Herndon, VA 22070 (703) 742-YOYO (9696)

Articles

Burger, Wolfgang. The Yo-Yo: A Toy Flywheel. American Scientist,
March/April, 1984. The most complete review of yo-yo science,
by its foremost investigator.

Hoffman, Abbie. Yo-Yo Power. Esquire, October 1970. Abbie Hoffman,
a former Worcester, Massachusetts yo-yo champ, talks about
a youth spent on one end of a yo-yo string.

Zuckerman, Edward. Quest for the Perfect Yo-Yo. Science Digest, July
1985. A description of Tom Kuhn and his amazing yo-yos.

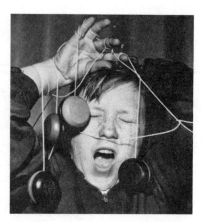

PHOTO CREDITS

page ii, top, Donald F. Duncan, Jr. , *bottom,* Culver Pictures, Inc.

page iii, Michael Petroske

page iv, Michael Petroske

page vii, Donald F. Duncan, Jr.

page 3, AP/Wide World Photos

pages 42 and 43, Donald F. Duncan, Jr.

page 44, The Bettman Archive

page 45, Stormi Greener

page 47, Bob Weaver

page 49, AP/Wide World Photos

page 50, UPI/Bettman Newsphotos

page 51, Michael Petroske

page 52, inset, NASA; *starfield,* Royal Observatory, Edinburgh

page 54, Owen Brewer

page 56, center, Library of Congress; *top right,* Staatliche Museen Preussischer Kulturbesitz, Antikenmuseum, Berlin

page 57, The Metropolitan Museum of Art, Fletcher Fund, 1928.

pages 60 through 69, Donald F. Duncan, Jr.

page 70, The Bettman Archive

page 75, AP/Wide World Photos

page 76, Culver Pictures, Inc.

pages 77 and 78, UPI/Bettman Newsphotos

page 79, AP/Wide World Photos

Books Available from Klutz Press

The Aerobie Book
The Bedtime Book
The Book of Classic Board Games
Boondoggle: A Book of Lanyard & Lacing
Braids & Bows   The Buck Book   Cat's Cradle
Country and Blues Guitar for the Musically Hopeless
Country and Blues Harmonica for the
Musically Hopeless
Draw the Marvel™ Comics Superheroes
Earthsearch: A Kids' Geography Museum in a Book
Everybody's Everywhere Backyard Bird Book
Explorabook: A Kids' Science Museum in a Book
Face Painting
The Foxtail Book
The Hacky Sack Book
The Incredible Clay Book
Juggling for the Complete Klutz
KidsCooking
KidsGardening
Kids Shenanigans
KidsSongs   KidsSongs 2   KidsSongs Jubilee
KidsSongs Sleepyheads
Kids Travel: A Backseat Survival Kit
The Klutz Book of Card Games
The Klutz Book of Jacks
The Klutz Book of Knots
The Klutz Book of Magic
The Klutz Book of Magnetic Magic
The Klutz Book of Marbles
The Klutz Yo-Yo Book
Make Believe: A Book of Costume and Fantasy
The Official Koosh Book
The Official Icky-Poo Book
Pickup Sticks
Stop the Watch: A Book of Everyday Olympics
Table Top Football
The Time Book
The Unbelievable Bubble Book
Watercolor for the Artistically Undiscovered

Free Catalogue

Filled with more Klutz books, yo-yos, harmonicas, juggling apparatus, unicycles, boomerangs and who knows what all, the Flying Apparatus Catalogue has got to be the only one of its kind anywhere. The catalogue is available free for the asking.

Name _____

Address _____

City/State _____

Zip _____

Y

Filled with more Klutz books, yo-yos, harmonicas, juggling apparatus, unicycles, boomerangs and who knows what all, the Flying Apparatus Catalogue has got to be the only one of its kind anywhere. The catalogue is available free for the asking.

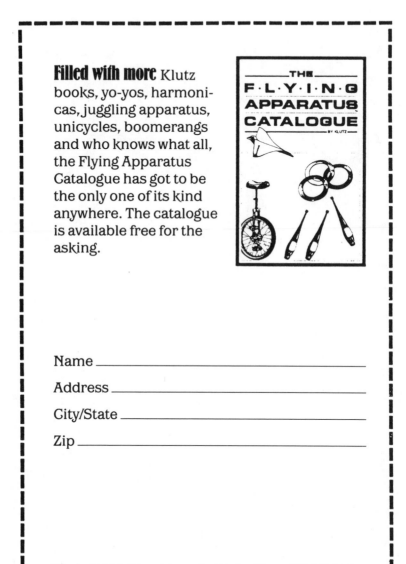

Name _____

Address _____

City/State _____

Zip _____

Klutz/2121 Staunton Ct./Palo Alto, CA 94306

Y

Filled with more Klutz books, yo-yos, harmonicas, juggling apparatus, unicycles, boomerangs and who knows what all, the Flying Apparatus Catalogue has got to be the only one of its kind anywhere. The catalogue is available free for the asking.

Name _____

Address _____

City/State _____

Zip _____

Klutz/2121 Staunton Ct./Palo Alto, CA 94306

Y